AMERICAN WAR BIOGRAPHIES

Robert E. Lee

E.J. Carter

Heinemann Library
Chicago, Illinois

Designed by Heinemann Library
Page layout by Lisa Buckley
Maps by John Fleck and Heinemann Library
Photo research by Janet Lankford Moran
Printed and bound in China by South China Printing
   Company Limited

08 07 06 05 04
10 9 8 7 6 5 4 3 2 1

Library of Congress Cataloging-in-Publication Data
Carter, E. J., 1971-
   Robert E. Lee / E.J. Carter.
      p. cm. -- (American war biographies)
   Summary: Profiles General Robert E. Lee, discussing his roles as an army engineer, soldier in the Mexican War, and superintendent at West Point prior to the Civil War, and service as a college president afterwards.
   Includes bibliographical references (p.) and index.
   ISBN 1-4034-5081-1 (lib. bdg.) -- ISBN 1-4034-5088-9 (pbk.)
   1. Lee, Robert E. (Robert Edward), 1807-1870--Juvenile literature. 2. Generals--Confederate States of America--Biography--Juvenile literature. 3. Confederate States of America. Army--Biography--Juvenile literature. 4. United States--History--Civil War, 1861-1865--Juvenile literature. [1. Lee, Robert E. (Robert Edward), 1807-1870. 2. Generals. 3. Confederate States of America. 4. United States--History--Civil War, 1861-1865.] I. Title. II. Series.
   E467.1.L4C29 2004
   973.8'1'092--dc22

                              2003021787

Acknowledgments
The author and publisher are grateful to the following for permission to reproduce copyright material:
pp. 5, 18, 43 Corbis; p. 7 Stapleton Collection/Corbis; p. 8 Richard Cheek/Stratford Hall Plantation/AP Wide World Photos; 11 Washington and Lee University, Lexington, Virginia; pp. 13, 1 17, 31 Hulton Archive/Getty Images; pp. 22, 29, 35 Library of Congress; pp. 26, 32 Medford Historical Society Collection/Corbis; p. 37 The Granger Collection, New York; pp. 38, 39 National Archives and Records Administration; p. 40 Virginia Historical Society, Richmond, Virginia; p. 41 AP Wide World Photos

Cover photograph by Library of Congress

The publisher would like to thank Gary Barr for his help in the preparation of this book.

Every effort has been made to contact copyright holders of any material reproduced in this book. Any omissions will be rectified in subsequent printings if notice is given to the publisher.

Some words are shown in bold, **like this.** You can find out what they mean by looking in the glossary.

Contents

1 Introduction

The nineteenth century was a relatively peaceful period in world history. Few horribly destructive wars like those of the twentieth century took place. An exception was the American Civil War (1861–1865), a bitter struggle between northern and southern states over the issues of **slavery** and **states' rights** in American society. After the Mexican War of 1846–1848 added new territory to the United States, debate raged over whether slavery would be extended to those areas, or would remain only in those states where it already was practiced. The South grew anxious that the North would eventually try to **abolish** slavery and destroy their way of life. When Abraham Lincoln was elected president in 1860, several Southern states broke away from the **Union** and declared the formation of an independent nation, the **Confederate** States of America. The war that followed was extremely brutal and bloody. Finally, in 1865, the South was defeated and brought back into the Union.

Robert E. Lee may have been the most talented general of the Civil War on either side. Before Lee took charge of the Confederate Army of Northern Virginia, the South was slowly inching toward defeat. Without his brilliant leadership, the South would never have survived the war for four full years. The Confederacy actually came close to winning the war because of Lee's victories. Eventually, however, the South was overwhelmed by the size and strength of the North.

Unlike many Civil War generals, Robert E. Lee was not a lifelong soldier. He attended the United States Military Academy as a young man and served in the U.S. army most of his life, but he worked as an engineer rather than a military commander. He built forts, dams, bridges, and roads all around the United States. His first experience in combat came during the Mexican War, and he did not lead his own troops until the late 1850s. Even Lee was surprised when he turned out to be such an effective military leader.

Lee's abilities in warfare were nothing short of amazing. He won victories against armies that often were twice the size of his own. At Gaines's Mill, Second Manassas, Fredericksburg, Chancellorsville, and Cold Harbor, he soundly defeated invading Northern forces. He even managed on two separate occasions to invade Northern territory in the hopes of winning a big battle that would bring the war to a close. Neither attempt succeeded, but history may have taken a very different course if they had.

Lee's success had many causes. He dealt well with other people, both **superiors** and **subordinates.** He never bullied his officers, but allowed them space to make their own decisions. He knew how to handle Jefferson Davis, the president of the Confederacy, by keeping him informed about the army's plans without allowing him to run the battles himself. But mostly his victories were due to his excellent ability to guess what the enemy generals planned to do, to position his troops in the best possible spots, and to know the right moment to take the offensive.

It was a difficult decision for Robert E. Lee to side with Virginia and the Confederacy. This portrait of General Lee was taken around 1863.

Lee's importance in history is not limited to his military feats during the Civil War. He was considered the perfect gentleman—brave, dignified, and modest—and he became a hero in the South. Even more than Jefferson Davis, the president of the Confederacy, Lee's legend lived on long after the war had ended. In the South he was thought of as highly as George Washington. Lee was uncomfortable with the idea of **secession,** but he believed it was his duty to serve his home state of Virginia. For that even Northerners respected and admired him.

Robert E. Lee's father was a colorful man named Henry Lee III, but to his friends he was known as "Light Horse Harry." Harry Lee fought alongside George Washington in the **Revolutionary War,** where he picked up his nickname. Washington even considered naming Harry head of the United States Army after he was elected president. In the 1790s Harry became involved in politics. He was elected governor of Virginia and later to the U.S. Congress. While governor he married a wealthy **plantation** owners' daughter named Ann Hill Carter. They had several children together, including Robert E. Lee, who was born on January 19, 1807. He was the family's fifth child. They lived on a large plantation owned by Harry and had a comfortable life.

But Harry Lee was also an unsuccessful land **speculator**— he bought land hoping the price would rise, and often it did not. After he left politics, his problems with money began to grow. Two years after Robert was born, Harry Lee was sent to **debtors' prison** for failing to pay his bills. He was set free after a year, but he continued to struggle. Because of these financial problems, the Lees had to sell off most of their land and were often forced to live as guests in other people's houses.

Eventually they moved into a small house in Alexandria, Virginia, 6 miles (9.7 kilometers) from Washington, D.C. Harry tried to make money by writing the **memoirs** of his war adventures, but he was not very successful. In 1813 Harry Lee went to live in the Bahamas to escape his troubles and to try to improve his health. His children never saw him again. He died in 1818 in Georgia on his way back to see them.

Henry Lee III was also known as "Light Horse Harry" from his service in the Revolutionary War. In his later years he was forced to sell off family land to pay his debts.

Lee's education

Fortunately, Ann Lee had inherited a small trust fund that her husband was not allowed to touch. She was able to provide her children with decent educations.

As a boy, Robert E. Lee attended Alexandria Academy. He was considered quiet, thoughtful, and very self-controlled. He received the usual education of the time. Students learned Greek and Latin and were expected to memorize a lot of ancient literature. But Robert also showed a talent for math. He learned arithmetic, algebra, and geometry and was known for his precision and his ability to reason out problems. This training in math would prove valuable in his military career.

When Lee was seventeen his family decided to send him to the United States Military Academy at West Point, New York. This was a great option for a family with financial problems because the tuition at **West Point** was free.

Lee met with the secretary of war, John C. Calhoun, and after some help from **influential** family members, he was able to win a spot at the academy. In 1825 he left his mother and family for the first time and traveled to New York.

Lee enjoyed his experience at **West Point.** He made several lifelong friends and quickly gained respect for military life. Discipline at West Point was very strict, but Lee had no trouble adjusting. To punish students for breaking the rules, the academy created a system of **demerits.** If a **cadet** acquired too many demerits he would be expelled. Most students had at least 50 demerits by the time they graduated, and many had more than 100. Lee, however, finished his four years of school without a single demerit. Unlike his father, Lee was also good with money. Many cadets went deeply into debt during their student life, but Lee actually had more money when he finished school than when he began.

Lee was also an extremely good student. He continued to excel at mathematics and even served as a tutor for other students after his first

This is the great house at Stratford Hall **Plantation**, where Robert E. Lee was born. It is located in Montross, Virginia.

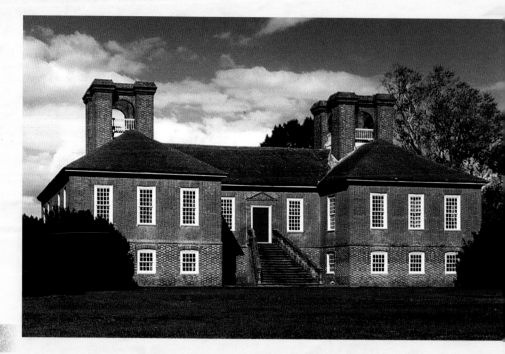

year. He also took courses in French, chemistry, physics, and military engineering. He had high test scores, and in 1929 he graduated second in his class. Lee was admired by everyone around him for his intelligence, his self-control, and his handsome physical appearance. Joseph Johnston, a fellow cadet who would also fight for the South in the Civil War, remembered "that no other youth or man so united the qualities that win warm friendship and command high respect." The stage was set for a very successful career.

Lee went home to be with his mother during the summer after his graduation. Ann Lee's health had begun to decline even before Robert left for West Point. He took care of her while she was ill, and she died in July. Lee was with her when she died, and it left a heavy impression on him that remained throughout his life. He also spent time that summer with Mary Custis, an old childhood friend. During the following year they kept in touch through letters and in the summer of 1830, he asked her to marry him. She, like Lee, came from a well-known Virginia family. Her father, George Washington Parke Custis, was the adopted son of George Washington. Mr. Custis inherited a 15,000-acre (6,070-hectare) estate from Martha Washington and built a mansion known as Arlington House, where Robert courted Mary Custis that summer. Mary was an only child and her father at first was hesitant to give her away. Finally he agreed to let the wedding take place. Their engagement lasted a year, and they were married on June 30, 1831.

West Point History

West Point was originally a fort built by George Washington's army along the Hudson River during the **Revolutionary War**. In 1802 President Thomas Jefferson created a school there to help support the army and educate officers. The person most responsible for developing West Point into a fine academic institution was Colonel Sylvanus Thayer, the "father of West Point." Thayer was **superintendent** of the school from 1817 to 1833. He knew that the growing country would have major engineering needs, and he insisted that engineering be an important part of the educational program. Most of the Civil War generals on both sides graduated from West Point.

3 Engineering

In between these summer visits to Arlington House to court and marry Mary Custis, Lee was working as an army engineer. The **Corps** of Engineers assigned him first to Cockspur Island near Savannah, Georgia. The army wanted to build a fort there and Lee's job was to help drain the marshy land by building a series of ditches and **dikes.** He also had to figure out how to supply the men doing the work with food and shelter. It was a frustrating job. When he returned to the area after his visit to Virginia in 1830, he discovered that thunderstorms had destroyed much of the work, thanks in part to a commanding officer who did not follow some of Lee's decisions. Lee tried to repair the damage, but soon he was reassigned to another project.

His next job was at Fort Monroe, in Old Point, Virginia. The fort had recently been built and Lee was brought in to help put on the finishing touches. He was happy to be in Virginia, close to Mary Custis. After their marriage she joined him at Fort Monroe.

Lee helped design moats, buildings, and **wharves,** and he tried to create an artificial island near Hampton Roads where another fort would eventually be built. This work was not especially satisfying to Lee; he felt he could be doing greater things. In 1834 he wrote to his brother, "I suppose I must continue to work out my youth for little profit and less credit & when old be laid on the shelf."

Before work on the fort was finished, Lee was transferred again. This time he became assistant to the chief of the Engineering Corps in Washington, D.C. The work was very hard and Lee did not enjoy the constant political arguing

nd power moves in Washington. Lee requested a new job, and the army sent him
) explore Ohio and Michigan during the summer of 1835. But Lee continued to
e frustrated with his career. Finally in the summer of 1837, Lee was sent to
t. Louis to work on a truly grand task. The Mississippi River was shifting away
rom the city. If it continued to move, St. Louis would have no way to load and
inload boats in its harbors. Lee was sent to change the direction of the river so
hat it continued to flow past St. Louis.

.ee spent some time studying the situation, then designed a plan to build a dam,
. dike, and a stone shield on one of the Mississippi's islands to keep the river
n course. Lee's plan was brilliant, but he felt the government needed to provide
nore money to make it workable. He also removed thousands of pounds of
ock from the river so that ships could travel down it more easily. But Lee never
eceived the funds he needed to complete his projects, and after four years, he
eturned to Washington.

)uring much of this period Lee had been separated from his family. By the time
te moved to St. Louis, he had three children—two sons, Custis and Rooney, and
t daughter, Mary. His family came to St. Louis for about a year in 1838–1839,
)ut they complained that
he weather was too hot.
.ee was very involved in
tis children's upbringing
tnd education, but his
ob forced him to spend
ong periods of time away
rom them.

'his portrait of Mary Ann
Randolph Custis Lee was done
n 1838. By that time the Lees
tad been married seven years
nd had three children.

4 War in Mexico

Between 1840 and 1846, Lee continued to work as an engineer, mostly around Fort Hamilton in New York City. The jobs were mostly boring and unchallenging compared to the task in St. Louis, but he was earning a good living and his family was growing. By 1846 he and Mary had four more children.

Suddenly, in 1846, the United States went to war with Mexico. Lee immediately requested to join the army, and he was sent to San Antonio, Texas, to join General John E. Wool's forces. The army began a long march south, covering 700 miles (1,126 kilometers) before reaching the city of Monclava. Lee's duty was mainly scouting. He would ride ahead on his horse and find the best paths forward, making sure no enemy troops were ready to attack Wool's army. Lee developed a liking for Mexican food and was impressed by the wolves that surrounded the camps every night.

Wool's army never encountered Mexican General Antonio Lopez de Santa Anna's forces like they expected. In

Winfield Scott

Winfield Scott was born in Virginia, and as a young man he studied and practiced law. When the War of 1812 broke out between the United States and Great Britain, he joined the army. He soon rose to the rank of major general, and for the next 30 years he led military operations in a variety of places throughout the United States. But he only became famous when he was placed in charge of the U.S. invasion of Mexico City. Scott completed that task successfully despite having to deal with disloyal **subordinate** officers and political **controversies.** In 1852 Congress promoted him to lieutenant general, the first person to hold that office since George Washington.

The Mexican army was forced to flee after the Battle of Cerro Gordo, which took place April 17–18, 1847.

January 1847, Lee was ordered to join General Winfield Scott, the commander of the American forces, in his attack on Vera Cruz. This would be Lee's first combat experience. On March 22 the bombardment of the city began. Lee was placed in a charge of a naval battery; he decided where to point the guns and when to fire them. The bombing last five days before the city surrendered.

The army moved on and defeated the Mexicans at the battles of Cerro Gordo, Contreras, and Churubusco on its way to Mexico City. Lee served as an advisor to General Scott and also occasionally led troops on special missions. On August 19 he fought two separate battles in a row, staying awake for 36 hours. Winfield Scott called it "the greatest feat of physical and moral courage performed by any individual in my knowledge."

In September 1847, Scott laid **siege** to Mexico City, with Lee advising him on geography, land, and plans. He also commanded a battery of guns firing on Chapultepec, a fortress guarding the city. Lee was slightly wounded, and at one point he fainted, but he recovered in time to see the U.S. army capture Mexico City. For his performance in these battles, Lee was promoted to colonel. After a life as a unsatisfied engineer, Lee suddenly discovered at age 40 that he was a very talented soldier.

5 Back to West Point

Lee left Mexico for home on June 9, 1848. After a brief vacation, his family moved to Baltimore, Maryland, where he worked on the construction of Fort Carroll. Life had returned to normal.

Then in 1852 Lee was named **superintendent** of **West Point,** the military academy he had attended as a young man. Lee was not entirely happy with this appointment, since he had no experience in the field of education. He reluctantly accepted the post.

Two of Lee's major tasks were enforcing discipline among the students and raising money for new buildings for the academy. Lee did not enjoy enforcing the rules and regulations. Many students with too many **demerits** asked to be let off and Lee had to decide who would be allowed to stay and who would be expelled. Often those with important connections received special treatment, and Lee was uncomfortable with these conditions.

There was one aspect of his new job that Lee enjoyed very much. He had access to the academy's library and he spent of great deal of time there reading books on military history and strategy. The **campaigns** of the French Emperor Napoleon Bonaparte, who ruled from 1799–1815, were the subject of many of these texts. Lee studied them closely. He had decided, thanks to his experiences in Mexico, that he was more interested in military life than in engineering.

In 1855 Robert E. Lee left the Engineering **Corps** of the army and was transferred to the **cavalry.** The army had established two new divisions to protect settlers in **frontier**

This photograph shows a group of guns at West Point on the Hudson River in New York. Lee was not entirely happy to come back to West Point military academy as its **superintendent**.

regions of the country. Lee was made second in command of the Second Cavalry in Texas. This was Lee's first experience in directly commanding his own troops. In the Mexican War he had been a **staff officer** as opposed to a **line officer.** That means that he planned strategy, went on scouting missions, and advised the generals, but did not directly tell troops what to do. Now he would have his own men for the first time.

In Texas, Lee's main duty was to prevent conflicts between white settlers and Comanche Indians who lived on a nearby reservation. Otherwise he had very little to do. He was again separated from his family. His children had grown up and he wanted to help them find careers and go to college, which was hard to do while he was away from home.

6 A Gentleman Farmer in Virginia

In 1857 George Washington Parke Custis, Lee's father-in-law, died. He left most of his land and his house at Arlington to his daughter Mary, and he gave smaller gifts to his grandchildren. It was Robert E. Lee's job to make sure these gifts were distributed properly. After the estate was settled, all of the Custis slaves were to be set free.

Lee has mixed feelings about **slavery**. He himself owned slaves, who worked as household servants, until at least 1846, when he apparently set them free. Despite this act, Robert E. Lee did not believe in human equality. He held negative opinions not only of blacks, but of the Mexicans and Native Americans he had met at other stages in his career. Even whites were not all equal in his view. He believed that a small group of educated and wealthy individuals from **elite** families should hold power and make decisions for everyone else. This was not an uncommon attitude among people from wealthy, well-educated families of the time.

On the other hand, Lee also believed that slavery was wrong, **immoral,** and bad for the United States. He once wrote, "Slavery as an institution, is a moral & political evil in any Country." Eventually, he believed, slavery should be **abolished,** but not too quickly. Too much freedom and **democracy** might lead to disorder. This was an attitude typical of the political party known as the **Whigs** during the first half of the nineteenth century.

But when it came to the slaves he inherited from his father-in-law, Lee had trouble setting them free, even though their owner had insisted on it. Custis had a lot of debts that needed to be paid off before the lands could be sold. Therefore, the slaves, who believed they were already free, were forced to work for several additional years. They had to work to raise money before they could be set free.

Lee took a leave of absence from the army to work on these problems. He did not enjoy acting as a **plantation** owner. But felt he had no other choice if he wanted to provide for his family's future. He brought the principles of military life to the plantation. To earn money, he hired some of the slaves out to neighboring plantations and other employers. There, they were forced to work under much harsher conditions than they had on the Custis farm. Lee also set to work repairing buildings, roads, and fences.

Arlington House was located in Virginia, across the Potomac River from Washington, D.C. This 1861 photograph shows it being occupied by **Union** troops.

He directed the planting, trying to make the farm more profitable than it had been in the past. The work was long, hard, and depressing. Lee wrote at the time, "I have no enjoyment in my life now but what I derive [receive] from my children."

Meanwhile, events elsewhere in the country were developing, which would change Lee's life. In Harper's Ferry, in western Virginia, a man named John Brown and about twenty of his followers took over a federal **arsenal** and held several hostages. John Brown was a passionate **abolitionist** who first became famous when he killed several pro-**slavery** individuals in Kansas. His raid on Harper's Ferry was an attempt to begin a slave **revolt** in the South, which he hoped would end slavery for good.

Lee was called on to lead the U.S. troops against Brown and his raiders. Lee was picked because he was living nearby. If Lee had not been caring for the Custis estate, he never would have been brought into the situation. He did

Lee led U.S. troops against John Brown and his raiders at the arsenal at Harper's Ferry. Once the Civil War started in 1861, **Union** soldiers destroyed buildings and supplies at the arsenal, which is shown here.

The Whig Party

Although Robert E. Lee was not involved in politics, he liked the **Whig Party**. The Whig Party developed in the 1830s in opposition to President Andrew Jackson's Democratic Party. The Whigs favored the creation of a national bank and high tariffs, or taxes, on foreign goods. Their supporters were often merchants and manufacturers. The two main leaders of the party were Daniel Webster of Massachusetts and Henry Clay of Kentucky. The first Whig president was William Henry Harrison, who was elected in 1840. They also won when Zachary Taylor was elected in 1848. When the Republican Party was created in 1856, it stole much of the Whigs' support, and the party no longer existed.

not even have time to put on a uniform, but Lee immediately took charge. Lee surrounded the arsenal with marines, offered Brown a chance to surrender and give up the hostages, and then ordered an attack. The troops easily overcame Brown's small group of followers, and as a result Brown was hanged in December 1859. This experience may have played a role in Lee's later decision to fight for the **Confederacy.** It had a major effect on the mood in the South. When Northern abolitionists began praising Brown's raid and calling him a saint, Southerners feared the North was determined about abolition. The idea of **secession** was discussed heatedly throughout the South. In February 1860, Lee returned to his army in Texas, but the bitter contest over slavery was far from over.

During these months, Lee reflected on his career. He was now in his 50s, his hair was turning gray, and he felt had accomplished very little. His salary was low and he had not advanced far in rank. Other **West Point** graduates had found good employment working for railroad companies, or had risen further up the army ladder. His old friend Joseph Johnston was now a brigadier general. Lee found himself bored in Texas and believed he had not been given credit for the work he had done with the Second **Cavalry.** At this low moment, his life and his fate were about to change dramatically.

7   The War Between the States

1860

November
Abraham Lincoln
elected president

1860–1861

December—February
Seven Southern states
seceded and formed
the Confederate
States of America

1861

March 13
Civil War began at
Fort Sumter

April 17
Virginia seceded

April 19
Lee resigned from
U.S. army

July 28
Lee assigned
to supervise
Confederate
troops in
northwest Virginia

1862

March 2
Lee returned to
Richmond to advise
Jefferson Davis

While Lee tried to keep busy in Texas, the United States wa.
moving toward civil war. In late 1860 and early 1861, seven
Southern states (South Carolina, Georgia, Florida, Alabama.
Mississippi, Louisiana, and Texas) **seceded** from the
Union after Abraham Lincoln was elected president.
Virginia was not among the original **Confederate** States.
Debate raged in Richmond, Virginia's capital city, over
whether to secede or to stay in the Union. In April 1861,
Lee was ordered back to Washington, D.C., to discuss the
coming war. He was offered command of the United States
Army after Winfield Scott recommended him for the job.
But Lee turned down the offer and declared that he would
follow Virginia. If his home state seceded, he would fight
for the Confederacy, and if it stayed with the Union, so

This map shows the status of states and territories during the Civil
War, which took place 1861–1865.

KEY — United States, 1861

Union States | Confederate States (slavery permitted) | Slave States (loyal to the Union) | Territories

would he. On April 17, a convention in Virginia voted for secession and two days later, Lee **resigned** from the U.S. army. Arkansas, North Carolina, and Tennessee also joined the Confederate **rebellion.**

Lee claimed that he did not believe in the right to secede from the Union. Nonetheless, his first loyalty was to his home state: "If Virginia stands by the old Union, so will I. But if she secedes (though I do not believe in secession as a constitutional right, nor that there is a sufficient cause for revolution), then I will follow my native State with my sword, and, if need be, with my life." The governor of Virginia named Lee head of his state's military forces, and Lee accepted. At this point in his life Lee still had never actually led troops in battle. But he was very impressive in person, with his tall height and distinguished manner, and he was known to be a master of strategy. People believed he was a great soldier and would be very valuable to the Confederacy.

In May the Confederacy moved its capital from Mobile, Alabama, to Richmond, Virginia. The Confederate president, Jefferson Davis, reorganized the Southern armies and placed Virginia's troops under the command of Confederate generals. Lee became an important advisor to Davis, and the two men developed a close relationship. Lee was especially involved in moving and supplying troops from his own state. In the Civil War's first major battle, at Manassas/Bull Run, a fourth of the Confederate soldiers came from Virginia, which suggests how well Lee had organized the Virginia army. The troops performed well, too. The Confederate armies led by Joseph E. Johnston and Pierre Beauregard smashed the invading forces under Union General Irwin McDowell and sent them fleeing back to Washington, D.C.

Joe Johnston

Joe Johnston was born in Virginia in 1809. He graduated from **West Point** in 1829 and had a distinguished career in the U.S. army. He was the highest ranking officer to resign from the army to join the Confederacy. After Johnston recovered from his wound at Seven Pines, he was sent west to supervise the armies of Pemberton and Bragg. He and Jefferson Davis often argued with one another. In 1864 he took over the Army of Tennessee and tried to stall Sherman's advance through Georgia. Davis again grew frustrated and removed him, and Sherman swiftly destroyed his successor. After the war, Johnston worked for railroad and insurance companies and served one term in Congress.

The Union army was forced to abandon this field hospital at Savage Station, Virginia. The army retreated in 1862 when Lee returned to the area.

Lee's first assignments

On July 28, 1861, Davis sent Lee to the mountainous region of northwest Virginia to supervise the Southern forces there. This was a important area. There were many **Union loyalists** in this part of the country. It was also an important area with many key roads, bridges, and mountain passes. Lee still did not command his own troops, but he advised the **Confederate** commanders in the area, led by William W. Loring, on ideas for attacking the Union forces. Lee tended throughout his life to avoid confrontation and conflict and so he relished his role as advisor. However, sometimes the generals did not do what he thought they should.

With Lee's encouragement, Loring planned to attack Northern troops at Cheat Mountain. The assault probably would have succeeded, but a **regiment** from Arkansas feared the Union position was too strong and retreated. This frustrating failure was followed by a similar lack of action at Sewell Mountain. A commander waited too long to attack, giving the enemy time to retreat to a safer position. Despite Lee's efforts, the Union armies still emained in northwest Virginia when he returned to Richmond in late October. These events brought Lee a bad reputation in the press. Some people believed e was too old-fashioned and refined to be a good general. Newspapers began eferring to him as "Granny Lee."

Advisor to the president

ee next traveled briefly to South Carolina to help defend the coast from a Union nvasion. The South had virtually no navy, and the North had surrounded it vith a naval **blockade,** preventing goods from leaving and entering. The Union uccessfully took two forts during the winter of 1861–1862, but Lee helped revent them from gaining access to the mainland.

3y March 2, 1862, Lee was back in Washington, helping Jefferson Davis deal with crisis in the Confederate army. Most soldiers had originally volunteered to serve or one year. Now their enlistments were expiring and many wanted to go home. f too many soldiers left the army though, the South would have little chance in he war. Lee helped write a conscription, or draft, law that required all males etween the ages of 18 and 45 to serve in the Southern army for three years. The ill passed the Confederate Congress on April 16. The bill angered some because before, wealthy **plantation** owners did not have to fight. However, without a draft, he army would have crumbled.

At this point, the North was recovering from its big loss at Manassas the previous ummer, and troops again streamed south to invade the Confederacy. Under the command of General George McClellan, the Northern army sailed down the Potomac River and landed on the Virginia Peninsula, directly east of Richmond. The army defending Richmond was led by Joseph E. Johnston, one of the heroes of Manassas. Davis and Johnston did not get along very well. Johnston was very ecretive and did not want Davis interfering in his plans. To Davis, Johnston eemed to be retreating too much as McClellan marched closer and closer to he capital.

ee was the **intermediary** who tried to get Davis and Johnston to communicate vith each other, while reducing the tension between them. Compared to other generals, Lee was not interested in getting a lot of credit and glory for himself, and he did not insist on always getting his way. Therefore, both Davis and ohnston trusted and respected him. Soon this confidence would be rewarded.

8   Lee Takes Command

By this time, McClellan's army had gradually moved almost to the edge of Richmond. Still Johnston hesitated. Finally, on May 31, Johnston attacked at Seven Pines/Fair Oaks, just south of the Chickahominy River. The battle was a **draw,** but it had one major consequence that would shape the rest of the war: Joseph E. Johnston was shot in the shoulder and could not lead his army until he recovered. His replacement was Robert E. Lee.

Lee's strategy

On June 1, 1862, Lee finally took command of his own troops, the Army of Northern Virginia. He immediately laid out his view of how the war could best be won. Lee knew that the North was much stronger than the South in terms of people, money, international support, and size.

The Confederacy moved its capital from Montgomery, Alabama, to Richmond, Virginia, in 1861. The defense of the capitals was a concern for each side, since they were so close together.

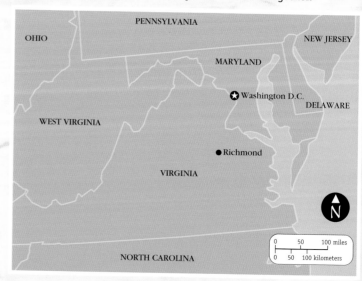

he longer the war lasted, the more likely it was that the **Union** would wear the Confederacy down. The only way to win, he felt, was to trap a Union army and destroy it. Perhaps a big victory would convince the North to give up rather than sacrifice money and lives in a long war.

Lee was a much better communicator than Johnston. He knew Jefferson Davis often tried to interfere in his generals' work, but instead of hiding his plans from the Confederate president, Lee constantly told him what he was thinking and doing. This strengthened Davis's trust in Lee and made him less likely to overrule his star general. Even when Lee's ideas seemed risky and dangerous, Davis generally let him have his way.

From the beginning Lee felt it was necessary to go on the offensive and invade the North through Maryland and Pennsylvania. But he still had to deal with McClellan and his 100,000 troops right outside Richmond. His plan was to send most of his army to McClellan's right **flank** and drive him away from the capital. Meanwhile General Thomas (Stonewall) Jackson, who had been winning big victories in the Shenandoah Valley in western Virginia, would march his troops in behind the Union army.

The Seven Days

The battle began on June 26, 1862, when McClellan attacked. The two armies would fight for the next week, in what became known as the Seven Days battle. The first two days ended in a **stalemate** with heavy Southern losses. But on the third day, at Gaines' Mill, Lee's forces broke through Union lines. The next day McClellan began to withdraw. Lee had managed to convince him that the Confederate forces were much larger than they actually were. McClellan moved toward the south, trying to reach the James River, while Lee pursued. But some of his forces were slow to move and he had trouble coordinating his generals. Lee mounted one final attack at Malvern Hill, and it was a disaster. Union troops mowed down row after row of Confederate soldiers. Lee had removed the threat to Richmond, but failed to destroy McClellan's army as he had hoped.

A second invasion

After the Seven Days, Lee reorganized his army. He made Stonewall Jackson and James Longstreet the leaders of the two major wings of the force, while several unreliable commanders were dismissed or reassigned. A. P. Hill and D. H. Hill remained in place as important **subordinates.**

But Lee did not have much time to relax. While McClellan's army was camped along the James River, 23 miles (37 kilometers) from Richmond, another large **Union** army began marching south. John Pope led the Union army on a bold offensive, living off the farms and fields around him rather than on supplies shipped from the north. Lee split his army in half, letting Jackson finish

Later in the Civil War, in 1863, Major General James Longstreet disagreed with Lee's decision to attack at Gettysburg, Pennsylvania.

battles behind Pope while Longstreet approached from the south. At Manassas/ Bull Run, the two sides again fought a major battle on August 30, 1862, and again the **Confederates** won. Pope was clearly outmatched by Lee even though Pope's army was bigger. Pope retreated to Washington.

The night after Second Manassas, Lee was riding his favorite horse, Traveller, when he fell off and sprained both of his wrists. For several weeks he was unable to write or to dress himself. But the injury did not hurt his aggressiveness. He believed the Confederates needed to follow up their victory with bold action. Lee's army was in no condition to attack Washington, D.C., which was defended by hundreds of thousands of troops. But he thought it would be a good time to invade Maryland. He wrote to Jefferson Davis, "we cannot afford to be idle, and though weaker than our opponents in men and military equipments, must endeavor to harrass, if we cannot destroy them."

Some residents of Maryland were pro-Confederacy, and both Davis and Lee believed they might welcome the Southern army as **liberators.** If they could convince the Marylanders to join the Confederacy, that would strengthen their cause tremendously.

ut even if they failed to conquer Maryland, simply showing that a Southern army was strong enough to invade a Northern state might convince the North that this long, difficult, and bloody war was not worth fighting. Maybe the Union would give up and allow the South to remain independent.

By September 7, Lee's armies had entered Maryland, and Lee issued a **proclamation** informing the local residents that the troops would not harm them or their property. He also drew up Special Orders No. 191, describing his attack plan. Several copies of the document were made and taken to the different sections of the army. But one of the copies was lost and fell into the hands of Union troops. Therefore George McClellan, who had by now left Virginia with his troops and returned to Washington, D.C., knew exactly what Lee planned to do. He attacked Lee's forces and pinned them on a group of hills west of Antietam Creek, near the town of Sharpsburg.

September 17, 1862, was the bloodiest single day of the entire Civil War. McClellan had a chance to destroy Lee's entire army, but Lee fought him off. The **casualties** were staggering: 10,318 on the Confederate side; 12,410 on the Union side. But the result was a **stalemate,** and during the night, Lee led his troops back across the Potomac River into Virginia. Lee's attempt to invade the North had failed, but it could have been much worse.

This is the proclamation Lee published when his army invaded Maryland:

To the People of Maryland:
It is right that you should know the purpose that brought the army under my command within the limits of your State, so far as the purpose concerns yourselves.
The people of the Confederate States have long watched with the deepest sympathy the wrongs and outrages that have been inflicted upon the citizens of a commonwealth allied to the States of the South by the strongest social, political, and commercial ties...
Believing that the people of Maryland possessed a spirit too lofty to submit to such a government, the people of the South have long wished to aid you in throwing off this foreign yoke, to enable you again to enjoy the inalienable rights of freemen, and restore independence and sovereignty to your State.
In obedience to this wish, our army has come among you, and is prepared to assist you with the power of its arms in regaining the rights of which you have been despoiled....
R.E. Lee

9 The South Gains Momentum

Once back in Virginia, Lee had to repair his army. His men were hungry, exhausted, and many had poor clothing, shoes, and weapons. Fortunately for Lee, McClellan did not chase him back into Virginia, and his troops had some time to relax and recover. By December 1862, his army, which had lost many men, was back up to 78,511 in size, thanks to new **recruitment** efforts.

Abraham Lincoln, the United States president, lost his patience with George McClellan. On November 7, 1862, he replaced him as commander of the **Union** Army of the Potomac with Ambrose Burnside. Lee was confident he could outsmart Burnside as he had McClellan, but he preferred fighting someone he knew. "I fear they may continue to make these changes till they find some one whom I don't understand," he said. Burnside's fighting style was actually similar to McClellan's, and Lee continued to win battles against the North.

Lee soon figured out that Burnside was crossing the Rappahannock River and planning to march through Fredericksburg, Virginia. Lee got to the town faster and set up a powerful defensive position. On December 13, Burnside's forces could not get through Lee's barriers. The battle turned into a slaughter. The Union lost 12,653 men that day and retreated in the night across the river.

By now Lee was celebrated throughout the **Confederacy** as a hero. Newspapers wrote endless articles about him, people from every Southern state sent him gifts, and admiration of him almost reached the point of worship. But Lee had little time to enjoy the glory. Not only was he

The Battle of Antietam was the bloodiest day of the Civil War, with both sides suffering heavy losses. Because Lee retreated, the North called it a victory. Lincoln had been waiting for a Union victory before issuing his **Emancipation Proclamation.**

thinking about his battles, but his personal life was difficult. Union armies had possessed or destroyed the property he had inherited from his father-in-law, and most of his wealth was gone. He rarely got to see his family during the war, except when he bumped into one of his sons serving in his own army. All of his sons survived the war, but several were wounded or captured. The death of his daughter Annie from **typhoid fever** in 1862 was especially painful. He wrote to another daughter that Christmas, "But what a cruel thing is war. To separate families, and to separate and destroy families and friends, and to mar the purest joys and happiness God has granted us in this world."

On December 28, 1862, Lee **emancipated** the slaves he had inherited from his father-in-law, George Washington Custis. This was not as noble a gesture as it seems. Most of the slaves had already been freed by invading Union armies, and the five year grace period that Custis's will gave Lee was expiring anyway. Furthermore, on January 1, 1863, Abraham Lincoln issued the **Emancipation Proclamation.** He declared all slaves in rebellious states to be immediately free. From this point forward, the war was fought not just to prevent the South from **seceding,** but to end the practice of **slavery** in the United States.

That winter was extremely cold. Though no fighting took place, in March 1863, Lee grew very ill. It was probably a heart condition, which he would suffer from for the rest of his life. He had little time to get well before the **Union** began its spring **campaign.** After the disaster at Fredericksburg, Burnside was replaced with General Joseph Hooker, who now led the North back into Virginia. Hooker's army had 133,868 men, more than twice as many as Lee commanded. The two armies fought at Chancellorsville, where Hooker took up a defensive position.

Lee learned through a scout that Hooker's right **flank** was very weak. Stonewall Jackson suggested leading his men secretly around Hooker's forces to attack that flank. It was a daring move because it left Lee with very few men to hold off Hooker's huge army. On May 2 Jackson began his long 14-mile (22.5-kilometer) march. When he finally attacked the flank, Lee sent the whole army forward. Jackson's move was a tremendous

Thomas "Stonewall" Jackson

Thomas Jackson was born in 1824 in Virginia. He attended **West Point** from 1842 to 1846, where he was known as a hard-working student. He fought in the Mexican War and continued to serve in the military until 1851. He then became a professor of **artillery** tactics at the Virginia Military Institute. He mastered military strategy in his years as a teacher, and when the Civil War broke out, he quickly distinguished himself. At the Battle of Bull Run/Manassas (July 21, 1861), Jackson became known as Stonewall, when a general said, "There is Jackson standing like a stone wall." Jackson died of pneumonia several days after being shot accidentally by his own men.

This painting shows the last meeting between Confederate army Generals Stonewall Jackson (left) and Robert E. Lee (right). Jackson was mistakenly shot and fatally wounded by his own men during the Battle of Chancellorsville.

success and confused Hooker's forces. The fighting continued over the next few days, but on May 6, Hooker retreated back over the Rappahannock River.

But there was a dark side to this **Confederate** victory. As night fell on May 2, 1862, Stonewall Jackson urged A. P. Hill's division forward to cut off Hooker's retreat. As the two **artillery** began firing at one another, Jackson and his aides scrambled out of harm's way. Just then, a group of Confederate soldiers from North Carolina fired directly across their path. Jackson was hit by four bullets. He was rushed to a medical tent where his left arm was **amputated.** A few days later he caught **pneumonia** and on May 10, he died. He had been Lee's best general and despite the string of victories the Southern army had enjoyed, the road forward would only grow more difficult.

10 Gettysburg

Jackson's death led to a major reorganization of the Army of Northern Virginia. Lee now divided it into three **Corps** led by James Longstreet ("Old War Horse"), Richard S. Ewell ("Old Bald Head"), and A. P. Hill. J. E. B. Stuart continued to lead a **cavalry** division. The loss of Jackson made Lee's task much more difficult because he relied heavily on his **subordinate** officers. Lee did not like to have to give orders to his generals. He made recommendations and usually they followed them. He needed officers he could rely on. Lee also was not the kind of commander who personally led troops in the field. He carefully positioned his forces, then allowed his generals to make adjustments as the battle proceeded. Meanwhile, Lee observed from afar, or rode his horse back and forth until he could figure out what was going on.

Lee still believed that the only way the South could win was by beating the North in one final blow. He wanted to follow up the tremendous victories of the spring of 1863 with another assault on U.S. territory. This time he would drive through Maryland to Pennsylvania. On June 25 Lee crossed the Potomac River and entered hostile territory. By July 1 his armies had concentrated at Gettysburg, with the North closing in quickly. Lee was up against yet another new enemy commander: Hooker had been replaced by George Gordon Meade.

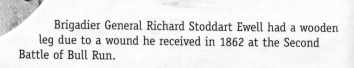

Brigadier General Richard Stoddart Ewell had a wooden leg due to a wound he received in 1862 at the Second Battle of Bull Run.

decisive battle

he two sides faced each other in the shape of a giant fishhook. Longstreet's Corps
essed east against the **Union** lines, while Ewell's curved around to the north.
eade held a key high spot called Cemetery Hill, and Lee believed it was key that
e capture this. Ewell delayed, though, and soon the North's grip on the hill was
o strong. Lee also argued with another of his lead generals, James Longstreet.
ongstreet wanted to wait for Meade to attack, while Lee insisted that the
onfederates take the offensive. Instead of following Lee's orders, Longstreet
esitated. Lee had planned for him to attack at dawn on July 2, but in fact it was
P.M. before his troops went into action. The Confederate offensive was not very
ell organized and therefore not very successful.

he next day fresh troops under George E. Pickett again attacked the Union lines.
few of them broke through, but eventually the charge failed. Meade had held off
e Confederate assault, and two nights later, Lee moved his men back to Virginia.
is army had suffered at least
0,000 **casualties.** The battle
f Gettysburg was Lee's best and
robably last chance to win the war.
e never again took his army into
orthern territory.

he loss at Gettysburg took away
ome of Lee's celebrity. Many
outhern newspapers criticized
im and accused him of making
iistakes. Lee felt his army had
one the best it could. In a letter
Davis he wrote, "I still think if
ll things could have worked
gether it [victory] would have
een accomplished." But stung by
e criticism, he volunteered to
esign his position. Davis refused
ven to consider it.

From Lincoln's speech delivered at
Gettysburg after the battle:
> Four **score** and seven years ago
> our fathers brought forth on this
> continent, a new nation,
> conceived in Liberty, and
> dedicated to the proposition that
> all men are created equal. Now we
> are engaged in a great civil war,
> testing whether that nation or any
> nation so conceived and so
> dedicated, can long endure. We
> are met on a great battlefield of
> that war. We have come to
> dedicate a portion of that field,
> as a final resting place for those
> who here gave their lives that that
> nation might live.

11 The Tide Turns

Along with anger in the press, Lee also had to deal with exhaustion among his troops. Many soldiers **deserted** after Gettysburg, and to recover troops, Lee had to use a mixture of threats and **pardons.** Lee also had to worry about the war in other parts of the country. Until now most of the important fighting had taken place in Virginia and neighboring states, but after Ulysses S. Grant's victory in Vicksburg in July 1863, the **Union** began threatening the **Confederacy** in the west. The Army of Tennessee was in trouble, and Davis wanted Lee to lead it. Lee refused because he knew nothing of either the troops or the territory, and he believed he would be more effective in Virginia. He did allow Davis to send Longstreet and his men to support the army in Tennessee. That meant Lee's forces were down to 46,000 men and could not pose much of a threat to the North.

During the fall of 1863, Meade again entered Virginia and looked for ways to attack Lee. To protect his shrunken army, Lee began to make more use of **trench warfare.** When his troops dug **embankments** in the ground they could easily hold off a much larger invading force. In what became known as the Mine Run **Campaign,** the two armies tested each other out, but no major conflict took place. Meade again retreated behind the Rapidan River to set up camp for the winter, leaving Lee frustrated that he had not been able to defeat him.

A new opponent

The following spring brought more changes. The Union won huge victories in Tennessee and now threatened the

Trench warfare allowed a defensive position to be held more easily for a longer period of time. These trenches were used by the Confederates to protect the city of Petersburg, Virginia,

Southern states of Georgia and Alabama. Ulysses S. Grant became general-in-chief, and he joined Meade with the Army of the Potomac. In May 1864, Grant led a new assault on Virginia. A full month of almost continuous fighting would follow, including some of the most intense battles of the entire war.

The first encounter occurred near Wilderness, Virginia. Through dense foliage and rough terrain the two sides hammered at each other, but neither side gained ground. James Longstreet, who had rejoined Lee, was shot by his own soldiers, just as Jackson was a year earlier. On May 7, instead of restarting the attack, Grant slipped his army through the woods and brought them south to Spotsylvania. On May 9 and 10, furious fighting again took place, especially at a weak spot in Lee's **fortifications** called the Mule Shoe. On May 11, Grant did not attack, and Lee assumed he was again on the move south. Lee moved some of his guns away from Mule Shoe to

Ulysses S. Grant

Ulysses S. Grant was born in Ohio and attended **West Point** from 1839 to 1843. He served in the Mexican War with Winfield Scott and later worked at an army fort in Oregon. He joined the Union army as a volunteer when the Civil War began and quickly started winning victories in the west. His conquest of Vicksburg in 1863 made him very popular in the North and by 1864 he was general-in-chief of the Union forces. He was elected president of the U.S. in 1868 and again in 1872. He is also the author of one of the most famous **memoirs** in American literature.

prevent Grant from running around him. But Grant surprised him by attacking the next day at Mule Shoe. Without the guns in place, the **fortifications** gave way and Lee had to retreat, building new trenches behind the old line. During the battle, Lee lost another prized general when J. E. B. Stuart was killed.

After several more days of brutal fighting, Grant again moved his troops to the south and to the east. At the Battle of Cold Harbor, Grant tried to divide Lee's army in half and rush to Richmond. The result was a disaster and Northern troops were defeated badly. By this time, Grant and Lee had each lost nearly half of their armies to **casualties** in some truly vicious fighting. The two armies had been battling now for an entire month.

Following a bloody battle like this, the losing side usually offered a **truce** that would allow each army to collect its wounded soldiers still stranded on the battlefield. On June 5, 1864, Grant suggested a cease-fire without sending the customary flag of truce. Lee refused and demanded that Grant admit his side had lost the battle. By the time they reached an agreement, only two soldiers still remained alive on the battlefield.

Siege at Petersburg

After his defeat at Cold Harbor, Grant decided to move his army yet again. On June 12 he marched past Richmond and neared the city of Petersburg. Lee and Grant both knew that Petersburg was key to the defense of Richmond, because important rail lines passed through it. If Grant cut those off, Richmond would not survive. The two sides again settled into **trench warfare** on the southern edge of Petersburg. This time, the **siege** would last many months.

On July 30 the **Union** tried to break through the trenches by digging a hole underground and setting off dynamite beneath the **Confederate** positions. The blast left a huge crater in the earth, and as Grant's troops charged forward, they fell into this crater. After this catastrophe the North was content to stay put in its trenches, gradually trying to wear the Confederates down. On August 9 the South tried a trick of its own by planting explosives on a **Union** ship. The bomb killed 43 men on board.

Over the next few months the armies fought occasionally, but no major battles took place. Even though the situation looked difficult, many in the South had come to think of Lee as a magician who could get his army out of any situation. Lee himself, though, knew that Grant's forces were growing bigger and bigger by the day, while his army was having trouble providing food and supplies to its soldiers.

As Grant's forces grew and Lee's supply lines were threatened, a strong Union attack seemed sure. Eventually Lee's army was forced to retreat and was finally surrounded. This painting shows the famous scene of Lee's surrender to Grant at Appomattox.

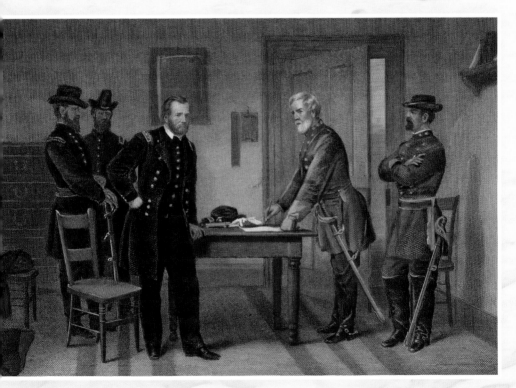

Lee met Grant in the McLean House in Appomattox Court House, Virginia, where he surrendered the main Confederate army.

Defeat and surrender

Finally on March 29, 1865, the North began a major assault. Grant attacked Lee's right **flank,** capturing and tearing up important railroads. When this charge succeeded, the whole army moved forward. By April 2 it had broken through Lee' trenches and sent his army into retreat. Lee at first hoped Grant would let him get away. He wanted to march further south to join Joseph E. Johnston and his Army of the Tennessee. His biggest problem, however, was how to feed and supply his hungry troops. With so many rail lines destroyed, and the surrounding countrysid destroyed, it was difficult to provide food for the soldiers. Lee began moving west, hoping that he would find rations at Amelia. He arrived and found nothing. He continued toward Lynchburg, still expecting trainloads of food to meet his army. But **Union** forces caught up with him at Saylor's Creek and destroyed divisions led by Ewell and Richard H. Anderson.

By April 7 Lee's army was nearly surrounded. He received a note on that day from Grant, proposing the surrender of the **Confederate** troops. Lee was not quite ready to give up. He mounted one last assault under John B. Gordon. When it failed he said to his aides, "Then there is nothing left me but to go and see General Grant, and I would rather die a thousand deaths." For Lee and his army, the war was over.

Grant and Lee met in a famous scene at the Appomattox Court House, where Lee officially surrendered. Grant promised that Lee's men would not be punished for their actions by the U.S. government and that they would be allowed to keep the personal possessions they brought with them to war, including their horses and mules. Lee said, "This will have the best possible effect upon the men . . . It will be very gratifying, and will do much toward conciliating our people." Lee had never been enthusiastic about **secession,** and he now hoped the two sides could quickly resolve their differences and become one nation again.

Shortly after his surrender in 1865, Robert E. Lee was photographed in Richmond by Mathew Brady. Brady took many famous photographs during the Civil War.

12 Life After War

There was nothing left for Lee to do but return to his family. His wife, two daughters, and two sons were living in Richmond, and a third son would soon arrive. His children would pursue their own careers, but Lee needed to figure out how to provide for himself and his wife, since most of their possessions had been lost or destroyed durin; the war.

Lee also worried about his own safety and freedom. After Abraham Lincoln was shot on April 14, 1865, some Northerners called for revenge. On June 7 a **grand jury** charged Lee with **treason.** Eventually the charges would be dropped, thanks to Ulysses S. Grant. Grant promised that those who surrendered would not be accused of committing crimes against the United States and would be allowed to return to their normal lives.

This photograph is of Robert E. Lee when he was president of Washington College.

Confederate General Robert E. Lee was photographed here on his horse, Traveller, during the Civil War. Lee was very fond of Traveller, whom he rode even after the Civil War.

A new job

In August 1865 Lee's professional problems were solved, too. The board of directors of Washington College in Lexington, Virginia, elected him as their president. Lee was not eager to teach at the school, but was interested in doing whatever he could to improve its condition. The college was in very bad shape. It had been plundered by **Union** troops and many of its buildings were damaged. Very few students or professors remained. After giving it some thought, Lee accepted the post, which he held for the rest of his life.

Still riding his favorite horse, Traveller, Lee moved to Lexington on September 15, 1865. He gradually came to enjoy the job. He attempted to improve the curriculum by offering courses in agriculture and the mechanical arts, as well as science, math, languages, and literature. Lee created the college's law school and began offering journalism courses, the first in that field to be offered in the United States. He was also very effective when it came to raising money to improve the campus. Cyrus Mc Cormick, the inventor of the **reaper,** donated $350,000. Lee helped put up new buildings and repair the old ones. He even designed the university's new chapel.

He also grew close to the students, and he even took an interest in disciplinary issues, which he had hated so much while he was **superintendent** at **West Point.** Over the next five years he did what he could to improve relations between Northerners and Southerners, and to minimize tensions between blacks and whites. The college quickly recovered from the damages of war and by the late 1860s, it was attracting students and money like never before. Lee's fame, along with his efforts on behalf of the school, played a big role in this **prosperity.**

The legend of Robert E. Lee

In 1870 Lee's health began to fail. His heart problems had never disappeared, and now they grew worse. He took a series of trips around the South that year, hoping to recover. Wherever he went he was greeted by huge crowds of adoring fans.

In the fall Lee returned to Lexington and attempted to go back to work. In October 1870, however, he suffered a stroke, and he died on October 12. Three days later, thousands gathered for his funeral, and he was buried in a vault in the Washington College chapel.

With his death a new stage of Lee's history began. He was transformed in the minds of many Southerners into an almost divine figure. Even though he was not enthusiastic about the idea of **secession,** Lee had sacrificed almost

Robert E. Lee holds an important place in the right-center of this image of Southern commanders in the Civil War. Also shown are Jefferson Davis, James Longstreet, J. E. B. Stewart, Stonewall Jackson, Joseph Johnston, P. G. T. Beauregard, and two unidentified commanders.

everything he owned to the cause. In many ways Lee led a very modest life. He spent most of his time in engineering projects and did not develop a taste for military service until later in life. He was not very interested in politics and was not remarkably ambitious. These qualities made his war heroism even more appealing to many people in the years after his death. But what really impressed people about Robert E. Lee was the dignified way he carried himself. He was polite, gracious, and selfless, and even in defeat he continued to exhibit these qualities.

Timeline

January 19, 1807	Robert E. Lee born at Stratford **plantation** in Virginia
June 1825	Lee began studying at the United States Military Academy at **West Point** (graduated 1829)
November 1829	Lee traveled to first job near Savannah, Georgia
May 7, 1831	Lee reported for work at Fort Monroe, Virginia
June 30, 1831	Lee and Mary Custis married
November 1834	Lee became assistant to the chief of the Engineering Department in Washington, D.C.
June 1837	Lee traveled to new job in St. Louis, Missouri
October 1840	Lee returned to Washington, D.C.
February 10, 1846	Mildred Childe, the seventh and final Lee child, was born
1846–1848	Mexican War
1852–1855	Lee was **superintendent** of West Point
1855–1860	Lee joined the Second **Cavalry** in Texas
November 1859	John Brown's **siege** at Harper's Ferry
April 19, 1861	Lee **resigned** from U.S. army
July 28, 1861	Lee sent to supervise forces in northwest Virginia
June 1, 1862	Lee takes command of the Army of Northern Virginia
June 26–July 2, 1862	The Seven Days battle
September 17, 1862	Battle of Antietam/Sharpsburg
December 13, 1862	Battle of Fredericksburg
May 2–6, 1863	Battle of Chancellorsville
July 1–3, 1863	Battle of Gettysburg
May–June 1864	Battles of Wilderness, Spotsylvania, Cold Harbor, and Petersburg
November 4, 1864	Abraham Lincoln reelected president

March 29, 1865	Ulysses S. Grant's spring offensive began
April 9, 1865	Lee's surrender to Grant at Appomattox
September 1865	Lee became president of Washington College in Lexington, Virginia
October 12, 1870	Lee died in Lexington, Virginia

Further Reading

Brewer, Paul. *The American Civil War.* Chicago: Raintree, 1999.

Isaacs, Sally Senzell. *America in the Time of Abraham Lincoln (1815–1869).* Chicago: Heinemann Library, 1999.

Naden, Corinne J. and Rose Blue. *Why Fight? The Causes of the American Civil War.* Chicago: Raintree, 2000.

Smolinski, Diane. *Key Battles of the Civil War.* Chicago: Heinemann Library, 2001.

Smolinski, Diane. *Soldiers of the Civil War.* Chicago: Heinemann Library, 2001.

Weber, Michael. *Civil War and Reconstruction.* Chicago: Raintree, 2000.

Glossary

abolish officially put an end to something; an abolitionist was a person who demanded that slavery be ended in the South

amputate cut off a person's body part, usually because it is diseased or damaged

arsenal building where weapons and military supplies are stored

artillery powerful guns that are mounted on wheels or tracks or part of an army that uses large guns

blockade closing off an area to keep people or supplies from going in or out

cadet student in a military academy

campaign series of actions organized over a period of time in order to achieve or win something

casualty person wounded or killed during a battle

cavalry soldiers who ride horses

Confederacy eleven Southern states that seceded from the United States between 1860 and 1861; a Confederate is a supporter, citizen, or soldier of the Confederacy

controversy long or heated discussion about something that people have a great difference of opinion about

corps group of military officers and soldiers

debtors' prison place where people who owe and cannot repay money are held

demerit mark against someone, usually for doing something wrong

democracy government by the people in which majority rules

desert abandon the army

dike high wall or dam that is built to hold back water and prevent flooding

draw when both sides of a competition are even

elite group of people who have special advantages or privileges

emancipate free a person or group from slavery or control

Emancipation Proclamation order issued by U.S. President Abraham Lincoln on January 1, 1863, that freed the slaves of the Confederate states in rebellion against the Union

embankment long, low, earth structure built to carry a railroad, road, etc.; high bank at the sides of a river built to keep it from flooding

flank far right or left end of an army's line of troops

fortification building strengthened against attack

frontier border between two countries; edge of the settled part of a country

grand jury group of people that meet to decide if there is enough evidence to try someone for a crime

immoral unfair; without a sense of right or wrong

influential having the power to change or affect someone or something

intermediary person who settles arguments between two sides

liberator someone who frees another

line officer military leader who directly command troops

loyalist someone who remains loyal to a particular cause; during the American Civil War, a loyalist was someone who remained loyal to the Union

emoir story of a person's experiences and life

ardon forgive or excuse someone; to release someone from punishment

lantation large farm on which crops are tended by laborers who also live there

neumonia serious disease that makes breathing difficult

roclamation public announcement

rosperity state of being successful

:aper machine used to cut or clear grain or crops

:bellion struggle against the people in charge of something

:cruit find new members; one of those new members is called a recruit

:giment military unit

:sign quit or give up a job or other responsibility

:volt rebel against a government or an authority

evolutionary War war in which the thirteen American colonies won their independence from Great Britain. The war lasted from 1775 to 1783.

:cede separate from a larger unit, such as the Union

:ore twenty

:ege long assault on a town or fortress

:avery owning other human beings and forcing them to work

:eculator person who buys something and then quickly sells it to make a profit

:aff officer military leader who advises other officers, handles supplies, or performs other functions without directly commanding troops

:alemate position or situation that results in a deadlock, with no progress possible

:ates' rights view that the laws and customs adopted by the individuals states, including slavery, should not be interfered with by the federal government

:bordinate someone who is lower in rank or importance and can be told what to do

:perintendent official who directs or manages an organization

:perior higher in rank or position

:eason act of betrayal, such as against a country or government

:ench warfare when soldiers dig holes and build embankments to protect themselves; this makes it more difficult for the opposing army to move

:uce temporary end to the fighting

:phoid fever serious disease caused by germs in food or water

:nion another name for the United States of America; during the Civil War it referred to the states that remained loyal to the United States government

:est Point United States Military Academy at West Point, New York; Lee and most of the major Civil War generals attended the school

:hig Party political organization formed to oppose Democratic Party

Index